· VOICES ·
from
COLONIAL AMERICA

NEW YORK

1609—1776

MICHAEL BURGAN

WITH

TIMOTHY J. SHANNON, PH.D., CONSULTANT

NATIONAL GEOGRAPHIC

WASHINGTON, D.C.

Text copyright © 2006 National Geographic Society
Published by the National Geographic Society.
All rights reserved. Reproduction of the whole or any part of the contents without written permission from the National Geographic Society is strictly prohibited. For information about special discounts for bulk purchases, please contact National Geographic Books Special Sales: ngspecsales@ngs.org

John M. Fahey, Jr., *President and Chief Executive Officer*
Gilbert M. Grosvenor, *Chairman of the Board*
Nina D. Hoffman, *Executive Vice President,*
   President of Books and Education Publishing Group
Ericka Markman, *Senior Vice President, President of*
   Children's Books and Education Publishing Group
Stephen Mico, *Senior Vice President and Publisher,*
   Children's Books and Education Publishing Group

STAFF FOR THIS BOOK

Nancy Laties Feresten, *Vice President, Editor-in-Chief*
   of Children's Books
Suzanne Patrick Fonda, *Project Editor*
Robert D. Johnston, Ph.D., *Associate Professor and Director,*
   Teaching of History Program University of Illinois at Chicago,
   Series Editor
Bea Jackson, *Design Director, Children's Books and Education*
   Publishing Group
Jim Hiscott, *Art Director*
Margaret Sidlosky, *Director of Illustrations*
Jean Cantu, *Illustrations Specialist*
Carl Mehler, *Director of Maps*
Justin Morrill, The M-Factory, Inc., *Map Research,*
   Design, and Production
Margie Towery, *Indexer*
Rebecca Hinds, *Managing Editor*
R. Gary Colbert, *Production Director*
Lewis R. Bassford, *Production Manager*
Vincent P. Ryan and Maryclare Tracy, *Manufacturing Managers*

Voices from Colonial New York was prepared by
CREATIVE MEDIA APPLICATIONS, INC.

Michael Burgan, *Writer*
Fabia Wargin Design, Inc., *Design and Production*
Susan Madoff, *Editor*
Laurie Lieb, *Copyeditor*
Jennifer Bright, *Image Researcher*

Body text is set in Deepdene, sidebars are Caslon 337 Oldstyle, and display text is Cochin Archaic Bold.

LIBRARY OF CONGRESS CATALOGING-IN-PUBLICATION DATA
Burgan, Michael.
   Voices from colonial America. New York, 1609-1776 / by Michael Burgan.
      p. cm. — (Voices from colonial America)
   Includes bibliographical references and index.
   ISBN-10: 0-7922-6390-1, ISBN-13: 978-0-7922-6390-6 (Hardcover); ISBN-10: 0-7922-6860-1, ISBN-13: 978-0-7922-6860-4 (Library)
1. New York (State)—History—Colonial period, ca. 1600-1775—Juvenile literature. I. Title. II. Series.
   F122.B87 2006
   974.7'02—dc22

                                    2005022033
Printed in Belgium

CONTENTS

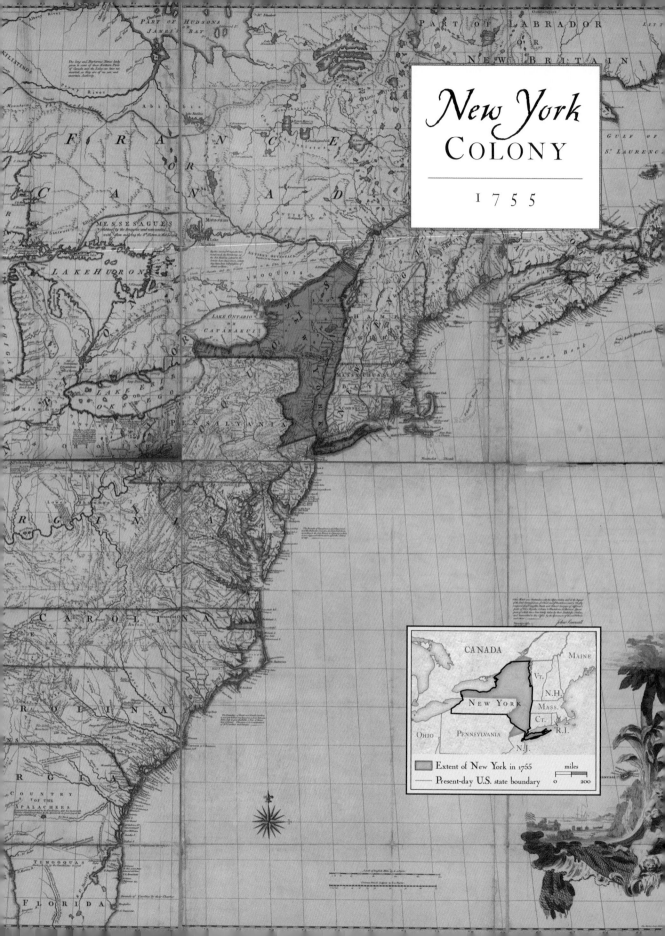

INTRODUCTION

by

Timothy J. Shannon, Ph.D.

This 1763 engraving shows the farmland that stretched to the walled city of New York. The large building in the center is King's College. Founded in 1754, it is now known as Columbia University.

It may be hard to believe now, but there was a time when the "wall" in Wall Street referred to a stockade built to protect Dutch fur traders and when "Yankees" were English newcomers, not baseball players. Native Americans and Europeans traded furs and beads made of sea shells with each other. Rich landowners lived on their Hudson

OPPOSITE: This historical map, created by John Mitchell in 1755, has been colorized for this book to emphasize the boundaries of the New York colony. The inset map shows the state's present-day boundaries for comparison.

River estates, with indentured servants and slaves laboring in their fields and homes. No one who visited this place in 1676 could have envisioned that it would become a center of population, power, and wealth a century later.

And yet, much about colonial New York reminds us of our modern world. Then, as now, New York was a mixing bowl of people with different ethnic backgrounds, who spoke different languages and practiced different religions. Iroquois, Delaware, and other Indian nations participated in the colony's economy and politics as business partners, allies, and occasionally enemies. Europeans from the Old World, displaced by war and poverty at home, arrived in New York seeking new freedoms and opportunities. In fact, there was such a diversity of backgrounds in colonial New York that no group was able to force its will entirely upon another. The stern Dutch governor Peter Stuyvesant had to support the rights of Jews and Catholics in his midst, at a time when religious tolerance was not the norm. The English eventually took over the colony, but they could not erase the religious freedom and ethnic diversity of the Dutch era.

This colony with its unique heritage also played an important role in shaping American liberties. The trial of New York printer John Peter Zenger was one of the earliest free speech cases in North America. A generation later, New Yorkers asserted their liberties by rioting against the notorious Stamp Act.

Other colonies may have been started on more high-minded principles than New York. New England had its Pilgrims and Puritans, whose religious convictions led them to the New World. Pennsylvania had William Penn and his Quaker-inspired "Holy Experiment" in peace and friendship. Peter Minuit's purchase of Manhattan from the Indians for the equivalent of $24 paints an entirely different picture, of a society where wheeling and dealing, not brotherly love, shaped people's ambitions and actions. And that remains New York's reputation today.

In *Voices from Colonial America: New York,* readers will enjoy learning about the many fascinating people who they will meet in these pages. Colonial New York was indeed a place distant from our own, but its legacies for modern America remain apparent in the opportunities we pursue, the values we share, and the liberties we embrace.

This silver Dutch coin (shown front and back), minted in 1623, was known as the Lion Dollar. It was a popular unit of currency in foreign trade not only in Dutch-founded New York but also throughout colonial America.

CHAPTER ONE

Colonial Beginnings

HENRY HUDSON'S EXPLORATIONS *lead the Netherlands to send traders to what is now New York. The Dutch meet two distinct groups of Native Americans—Algonquians and Iroquois.*

 n the 15th century, ships sailed from Europe to explore every corner of the world. The rulers of Europe wanted to trade goods, expand their empires, and lay claim to land in the New World—the Americas. By the late 16th century, the Dutch, the people of the Netherlands, were traveling to Asia, where valuable spices, such as pepper and nutmeg, grew on islands in the East Indies (Indonesia). Europeans prized exotic spices for their flavor.

OPPOSITE: In exploring the regions bordering the Hudson and Mohawk Rivers, the Dutch encountered Native Americans who lived in large bark-covered dwellings called longhouses. Some could be as long as 150 feet. Often several generations of one family lived together in one house.

In the spring of 1609, Henry Hudson of England sailed out of Amsterdam, the capital of the Netherlands. He worked for the Dutch East India Company, which controlled the Netherlands' trade with East Asia, where valuable spices came from. Hudson and his crew—half English and half Dutch—were aboard a new ship called the *Half Moon.*

English explorer Henry Hudson, hired by the Dutch East India Company to find a shorter route to Asia's spices, sailed south along the coast of New England into the mouth of the river that was eventually named for him.

Most European ships at the time sailed south, around Africa, to reach Asia. Hudson and some other explorers, however, believed that a river in North America could lead to a shortcut to Asia. Hudson headed west from Amsterdam across the Atlantic Ocean.

FIRST EXPLORATIONS

In September, the *Half Moon* pulled into a deep harbor. Hudson and his crew were the first Europeans to sail up the river that emptied into the harbor. They named the river the

North River. Today it is called the Hudson, in honor of the English explorer. The land they had reached would later become the colony of New York.

The *Half Moon* sailed up the river about 150 miles (241 km), reaching the site of modern-day Albany. Along the way, the Europeans met Native Americans, who greeted them from their canoes. Hudson and his men also went ashore at several spots and saw Indian villages. Robert Juet, an officer on the *Half Moon*, wrote a detailed account of the voyage. He described the contact with the Indians, saying they were *"seeming very glad of our coming."* Hudson and his men turned around when the river became too narrow. They sailed back down the river to the harbor and returned to Europe.

In Amsterdam, merchants were excited to learn that Hudson had brought back beaver pelts he had traded for with the Indians.

Before HUDSON

BEFORE HENRY HUDSON'S historic voyage, at least one other European reached what is now New York. In 1524, the Italian sea captain Giovanni da Verrazano had sailed into the same harbor Hudson entered in 1609. The surrounding land, Verrazano wrote, *"we suppose is not without some riches."*

Another European reached the northern part of New York in 1609. Samuel de Champlain, a Frenchman, left New France —what is now eastern Canada— to explore that region. A lake there was later named for him. For the next 150 years, the French would send fur traders and missionaries into northern New York.

Wealthy Europeans wore robes and hats made of fur from beavers and other animals. With the demand for pelts so high, trappers in northern Europe had killed most of the beavers there. The French were already trading with Native Americans in New France (eastern Canada) for beaver and other pelts. Now Dutch merchants saw a chance to build their own valuable beaver trade. Fur trappers and traders began to journey to the land Hudson explored, which was soon called New Netherland.

pelts—animal skins used to make fur clothing

THE DUTCH LAND OF
NEW NETHERLAND

TO THE DUTCH OF THE 17TH CENTURY, NEW NETHERLAND included all the land that Henry Hudson explored and the areas that trappers and explorers later found. The territory stretched from the Delaware River, in what is now Delaware, to the mouth of the Connecticut River, in what is now Connecticut. New Netherland also included modern-day New Jersey. The term "New Netherland" was first used in an official Dutch document in 1614. In this book, "New Netherland" refers primarily to the lands that became the state of New York.

In 1613, three Dutch ships reached one of the islands Hudson had seen in New Netherland's harbor. The Native

Americans of the region called the island Manhattos, which means either "island" or "hilly island." Today the island is called Manhattan. That winter, a group of Dutch sailors became the first Europeans to live on Manhattan. In the spring, one of the Dutch ships sailed up the Hudson River. On an island in the river near present-day Albany, the crew built a trading post called Fort Nassau. The fort lasted only a few years, but the Dutch returned to the region later, knowing how important the location was for the beaver trade.

THE INDIANS NEAR MANHATTAN

The Dutch traded with several different tribes of Native Americans. Around Manhattan and the lower part of the Hudson River, the Indians belonged to the Lenni-Lenape tribe. Later, settlers referred to them as the Delaware. The Lenape spoke three forms of the Algonquian language. Many other tribes in the northeastern part of what became the United States also

New Netherland boasted a thriving market for trade between Dutch colonists and Native Americans of the region. The Indians valued linen cloth, pots, pans and other iron goods, and novelties such as mirrors, which the colonists used as barter to get furs. The need to satisfy Dutch demand for furs eventually led to fighting among the Indians.

spoke forms of this language. Other Algonquian nearby were the Mahican and the Wappinger.

Native Americans first settled along the Hudson almost 11,000 years before the Dutch came. The first evidence of these Indians in what became New York City was discovered about 50 years ago. These people left behind stone knives and other tools. A scientific process called radiocarbon dating was used to determine the age of the tools. At first, the Indians of the northeast were mostly nomadic—groups of families moving together from one fishing or hunting ground to another. By the time the Dutch arrived, the Algonquian tribes spent most of the year in villages. Scientists called archaeologists suggest that the coastal Indians of New Netherland relied on fish and wild plants and animals for most of their food. Some of the Lenape farmed, raising corn, beans, and squash.

radiocarbon dating— the determination of the age of an artifact by measuring the amount of chemical carbon 14 it contains

archaeologists— scientists who study the past by digging up and examining items people used in their daily lives

INDIANS OF THE NORTH

Around Fort Nassau and into the west and north, a group of Indians called the Iroquois controlled the fur trade. There were five main tribes of the Iroquois: the Mohawk, Seneca, Cayuga, Oneida, and Onondaga. They spoke languages that were closely related and called themselves the

Hodenosaunee, which means "people of the longhouse." The Iroquois lived in houses up to 150 feet (46 m) long. The buildings were made of bark and had curved roofs. As many as 12 families might live in one longhouse. In some places, the Iroquois built high wooden walls, called palisades, around their homes. The walls kept out invading enemies while the residents inside prepared to defend themselves.

palisades—high wooden walls built to keep out enemies

Iroquois women grind corn, a staple of their diet, while a papoose, or baby, sleeps on a board that can be strapped to the mother's back for ease in moving from place to place.

TRADE WITH THE INDIANS

The desire for beaver pelts fueled the Dutch trade with the Indians. At first, traders could get the pelts they wanted from the Algonquian tribes. Over time, however, the supply of beavers around Manhattan began to run low, and most of the beaver trade shifted north, to the home of the Iroquois. They had easy access to forests and streams where plenty of beavers still lived.

The Dutch soon saw that the Iroquois valued wampum. They made belts out of the white and purple beads, which came from shellfish that lived along the coast of present-day New York and New England. Indians sometimes used wampum belts to pay debts or settle business affairs with outsiders. Because of this, the Dutch and later the English saw wampum as a form of money. The Algonquian who lived close to the Atlantic had a ready supply of the shells used to make wampum. The Dutch began trading such things as iron goods and cloth for the wampum. Then the Dutch traded the wampum to the Iroquois for their beaver pelts.

New England— name for the region east of New Netherland (New York) that was colonized by England

In the Netherlands, a new company was formed to control this growing trade with the Indians. In 1621, the Dutch government gave a legal document called a charter to a group of businessmen. The charter spelled out the land that the company would own and how it would operate.

charter—a legal document that spells out a person's or group's rights and duties

An existing company called The United New Netherland Company, which had been conducting business in the region around the mouth of the Hudson River, was made a part of the new company. This new company was called the Dutch West India Company. Its mission was to control the trade of The Netherlands. No Dutch citizen could trade with any place along the African coast or the American coast without the permission of the company. The Dutch West India Company had complete power in its chartered territory, and its leaders quickly began the process of turning New Netherland from a series of trading posts into a colony.

CHAPTER TWO

Building a Dutch Colony

THE DUTCH BUILD A COLONY *they call New Netherland. New Amsterdam is the capital, while Fort Orange is an important fur-trading post along the Hudson River.*

 hen Henry Hudson first sailed across the Atlantic, the Netherlands was one of Europe's newest nations. It had declared its independence from Spain in 1581. The Dutch, who were mostly Protestants, then battled the Roman Catholic Spanish to preserve their independence. In 1609, Spain and the Netherlands signed a truce in their war. The truce allowed the Dutch to trade freely around the world. The Dutch West India Company, seeing great value in the fur trade of

OPPOSITE: The first permanent Dutch settlement on Staten Island was established in 1661, after local Indians who didn't want their lands taken over by outsiders wiped out several previous attempts. This painting shows some of the tools and household necessities they had to bring with them.

North America, realized that it would need some colonists to go there and run trading posts.

NEW NETHERLAND'S ROOTS

Finding settlers for New Netherland wasn't easy, as the Netherlands' economy was strong. People had work, and they didn't want to risk their lives crossing the Atlantic and living in the wilderness. Finally, a group of Walloons offered to go to New Netherland. The Walloons were French-speaking Protestants who had fled the Spanish Netherlands. After working for the company six years, the colonists would receive their own land. The company would select a commander—later called a governor—to lead the colony, but he had to work with a council selected by the colonists.

AN IMMIGRANT COUPLE

TWO OF THE PEOPLE WHO sailed to New Netherland were Catalina Trico and Joris Rapalje. The two teenagers married in Amsterdam before beginning their journey. In New Netherland, they lived at Fort Nassau before moving to Manhattan and then Breuckelen. This village was just across the East River from Manhattan, on the western tip of what is now Long Island. (Today the village is better known by its English name, Brooklyn.) The Rapaljes' first child, a daughter named Sarah, is thought to be the first European born in New York.

In late spring of 1624, about 30 Walloon families reached New Netherland. They landed on what the Dutch called Noten Eylant—Nut Island. Today, this place in New York Harbor is called Governor's Island. Just over half of the families traveled up the Hudson River to a site near Fort Nassau, which had been washed away by snow and ice a few years earlier. There the settlers built a new trading post named Fort Orange. Other families were sent to build posts along the Delaware and Connecticut Rivers, while a group of eight men remained on Nut Island.

With the arrival of Walloons, French-speaking Protestants from the Netherlands, in 1624, the Dutch colony began to grow and prosper.

GROWING SLOWLY

In 1625, several more Dutch ships reached New Netherland, bringing more people, cattle, and supplies. Many of the new arrivals settled in Manhattan. The next year, Commander Peter Minuit bought Manhattan Island from a Lenape tribe, the Munsee. Minuit then began building a fort on the southern tip of the island. The Dutch settlers called their new capital city New Amsterdam.

This hand-colored woodcut shows an artist's interpretation of the purchase of Manhattan Island in 1626 by Peter Minuit. The Dutch commander, standing in front of his country's flag, offers a group of local Indians fine cloth, various tools, beads, and other goods in exchange for the land.

The Most Famous Purchase Ever?

FOR MANY YEARS, AMERICAN SCHOOLCHILDREN LEARNED that Peter Minuit bought Manhattan for the equivalent of $24. Of course, the Dutch didn't use U.S. dollars for cash—they used a currency called guilders. And in reality, Minuit did not give the Indians money. He traded goods worth 60 guilders for the land. In the 1800s, a historian suggested that 60 guilders would have been worth $24 at the time he wrote. No one knows for sure, however, what the guilders or the goods would be worth today. Minuit made a similar deal in 1630, when he bought Staten Island, which is now part of New York City. With that deal, Minuit traded *"kettles, axes, hoes, wampum, drilling awls . . . and diverse other small wares."* The Indians thought that they were merely giving the Dutch use of the land, and they continued to live on Manhattan and Staten Island.

During the next several years, the residents of New Amsterdam began raising crops, such as wheat, barley, oats, and beans, and traded with the Indians for pelts. In 1628, a Dutch writer reported that *"the population consists of two hundred and seventy souls, including men, women, and children."* The settlers lived *"in no fear, as the natives live peaceably with them."*

That year, however, the leaders of the Dutch West India Company were unhappy with their profits from New

Netherland. They decided not to invest more money in the colony. Instead, they would grant land to private citizens who would then pay for the settlement of new colonists. These wealthy landowners were called patroons. They received a plot of land along the Hudson River if they promised to find 50 colonists to settle on it. The Dutch West India Company kept control of Manhattan and some of the fur trade. The

patroons—Dutch term for wealthy citizens who owned large amounts of land and brought workers from Europe to take care of it

patroons hoped to farm and trade with other colonists in North America. They could also trade furs, but the furs had to be shipped to Europe through New Amsterdam, and the patroons had to pay a tax on each pelt. Some patroons traveled to the New World to manage their holdings themselves, while others remained in Europe and hired people to supervise their land holdings and business interests.

The first notable patroon was Kiliaen Van Rensselaer, who obtained land near Fort Orange. In 1630, the first settlers reached what was called Rensselaerwijck. These colonists were tenant farmers—they worked for Van Rensselaer and did not have the freedom to live beyond his lands. In

tenant farmer—one who farms land owned by another and pays rent in goods or cash

1640, Van Rensselaer wrote that he wanted his farms to *"make the country rich in grain"* that could be traded for sugar in Brazil. *"Then New Netherland would flourish."* Van Rensselaer, however, never traveled to the New World to see or manage his patroonship.

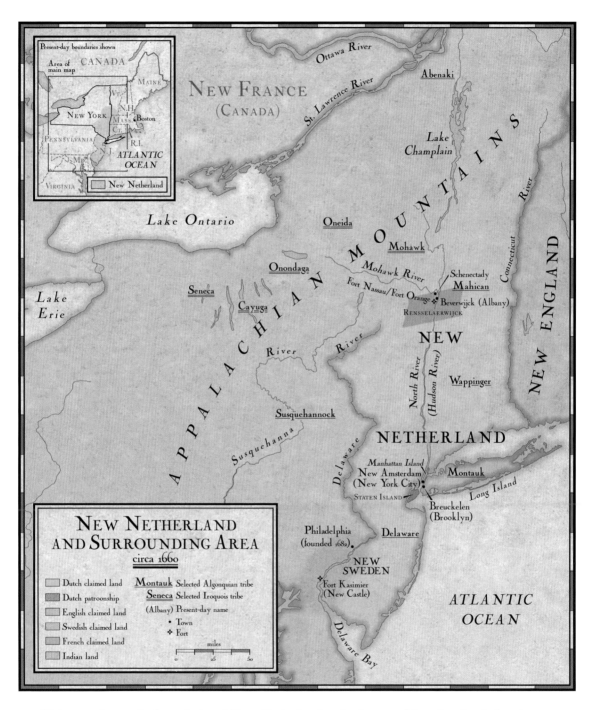

Present-day boundaries shown

Area of
main map

CANADA

MAINE

Vt.
N.H.
MASS.
CT.
R.I.
N.J.

NEW YORK

PENNSYLVANIA

MD.

VIRGINIA

ATLANTIC
OCEAN

New Netherland

Ottawa River

NEW FRANCE
(CANADA)

Abenaki

St. Lawrence River

Lake
Champlain

Lake Ontario

Oneida

Mohawk

Onondaga

Mohawk River

Schenectady
Mahican

Seneca

Fort Nassau/Fort Orange

Beverwijck (Albany)

Cayuga

RENSSELAERWIJCK

Lake
Erie

APPALACHIAN MOUNTAINS

Connecticut River

NEW ENGLAND

NEW

River

River

North River
(Hudson River)

Wappinger

Susquehannock

NETHERLAND

Susquehanna

Delaware

Manhattan Island
New Amsterdam
(New York City)

Montauk

Long Island

STATEN ISLAND

Breuckelen
(Brooklyn)

Philadelphia
(founded 1682)

Delaware

NEW
SWEDEN

Fort Kasimier
(New Castle)

ATLANTIC
OCEAN

Delaware Bay

NEW NETHERLAND AND SURROUNDING AREA
circa 1660

Dutch claimed land
Dutch patroonship
English claimed land
Swedish claimed land
French claimed land
Indian land

Montauk Selected Algonquian tribe
Seneca Selected Iroquois tribe
(Albany) Present-day name
• Town
✦ Fort

miles
0   25   50

This map shows the boundaries of New Netherland and what was New Sweden before it was
taken over by the Dutch in 1655. By 1660, the Dutch had established several towns, including the colony's capital at New Amsterdam, and private landholdings called patroonships.

LIFE FOR THE INDIANS

The arrival of Dutch settlers brought changes to both the Algonquian and Iroquois tribes. Starting in the 1620s and continuing for decades, the Indians ended some of their traditional ways as they traded with the Dutch and other Europeans. Hunters focused on killing animals that provided pelts the Europeans desired, rather than on killing game for food. The tribes then traded the pelts for European goods. The Indians also began to make clothes out of cloth they obtained from the Dutch, instead of animal skins and pelts, and they used metal tools, such as knives and axes, that the Europeans provided through trade.

The fur trade was not the only factor that changed life for the Indians. Along the coast, Indians put more time into making wampum, which the Dutch needed for trading with the Iroquois. During the 1650s, Indians on Long Island built a fort. In recent years, archaeologists examining remains from the fort think it might have been a wampum "factory," which produced large amounts of the beads.

The Dutch brought new goods that the Indians quickly learned to value. But the settlers and traders also brought diseases that the Indians had never been exposed to before. The deadliest was smallpox, which wiped out large numbers of Indians across North America. In 1656, a Dutch settler wrote, *"Before the small pox broke out amongst them, they were ten times as numerous as they are now."*

Native Americans trade fish and furs in New Amsterdam,
while the terms of exchange are discussed. In the background is a gibbet, a structure
from which the bodies of dead criminals are hanged from rings for public viewing.

BRINGING MORE SETTLERS

In 1639, the Dutch West India Company and the Dutch lawmaking body, the States General, approved a document called the Articles and Conditions. According to this document, all colonists who came to New Netherland would be allowed to trade fur and other items

VRYHEDEN

By de Vergaderinghe van de Negenthiene vande Geoctroyeerde West-Indische Compagnie vergunt aen allen den ghenen / die eenighe Colonien in Nieu-Nederlandt sullen planten.

In het licht ghegheven

Om bekent te maken wat Profijten ende Voordeelen aldaer in Nieu-Nederlandt, voor de Coloniers ende der selver Patroonen ende Meesters, midtsgaders de Participanten, die de Colonien aldaer planten, zijn becomen.

*Westindjen Kan sijn Nederlands groot gewin
Verkleynt s'vijands Macht brengt silver platen in.*

T'AMSTELREDAM,

By Marten Jansz Brandt Boeckvercooper / woonende by de nieuwe Kerck / in de Gereformeerde Catechismus, Anno 1630.

if they also farmed land. The colonists would receive as much land as they could farm, although they had to pay rent—one-tenth of the crops they produced. The next year, the company wrote the Charter of Freedoms and Exemptions. The charter provided that settlers who brought five adult relatives or servants received 200 acres (81 ha) of land, and the colonists gained greater control over their local governments.

Despite these changes, few people in the Netherlands felt the desire to go to North America. Other Europeans, however, liked the company's offer. Starting in the 1640s, more settlers, including English, Norwegian, and German citizens, slowly began to come to New Netherland. ✖

OPPOSITE: This page from the first pamphlet to be published about New Netherland, titled "Privileges and Exemptions," was designed to urge Dutch citizens to settle in the new colony, and mentions the great profits the Dutch West India Company was already making for the Netherlands.

CHAPTER THREE

Years of Conflict

CONFLICT ARISES AMONG THE DUTCH LEADERS *and Native Americans and Swedes, setting the stage for the English takeover of New Netherland in 1664. The colony is renamed New York. Dutch influence, however, remains strong.*

 hile the Dutch West India Company tried to bring new settlers to New Netherland, trouble was brewing with the native people of the region. In 1638 Willem Kieft took over as commander of New Netherland. (He and future commanders were also called governors.) The year after he arrived, Kieft placed a tax on the Indians. Kieft thought the tribes should help pay for Dutch troops stationed in New Amsterdam

OPPOSITE: As tensions between the Dutch and Native Americans increased in the 1630s, armed conflicts were common. This engraving shows the massacre of Algonquians that Governor Kieft ordered when the Indians refused to pay taxes to the colonial government.

and Fort Orange. The troops were supposed to protect the European settlers and the Indians from either hostile Indians or invading Europeans.

Governor Kieft (far right) meets with his advisers to discuss a solution to the ongoing fighting between Dutch settlers and their Indian neighbors over farming practices and taxes. In the end, he orders a war that almost wipes out the local Algonquian tribes.

Some Indian chiefs refused to pay the tax. Kieft soon launched a series of attacks on nearby Indians. David de Vries, a trader, complained that Kieft did not know the Indians or the colony and that *"commanders are sent here whether they be fit or not."* The wars with the Indians around New Amsterdam lasted until 1645. Some residents of Manhattan sent a letter to Dutch officials in the Netherlands. They described how their *"dwellings and other buildings are burnt; not a handful [of seeds] can be planted or sown this fall on the deserted places."* About 1,000 Indians died in the fighting.

In 1645, the Dutch signed peace treaties with various Algonquian tribes and the Mohawks. The settlers were most concerned about keeping good relations with the Mohawk and other Iroquois tribes. The Dutch would need the help of these tribes if they were to compete with the French in the fur trade in the future.

A NEW GOVERNOR

After the Indian wars, the Dutch West India Company replaced Kieft with Peter Stuyvesant. He wanted to strengthen the colony, as well as make money for the company. A 1650 report on life in New Netherland said, *"almost all the time from his first arrival . . . [Stuyvesant] has been busy building, laying masonry, making, breaking, repairing and the like."* Stuyvesant served as governor for 17 years. During that time, he made some political changes that helped the colonists. Towns on Long Island founded by English settlers began to ask for more local control, and the governor granted it. Some Dutch communities soon asked for and received the same right. Their local officials could make more decisions on their own, though they still needed the approval of the governor and his council.

Stuyvesant also took action that affected the Van Rensselaer family. In 1652, he took control of most of the land around Fort Orange. Before this, Rensselaerwijck had been mostly independent of the Dutch West India Company. The governor wanted the company to play a larger role in the beaver trade. Stuyvesant named the new town outside the fort Beverwijck—Dutch for "beaver district."

Peter Stuyvesant (center, with wooden leg), takes control of land around Fort Orange and orders the establishment of Beverwijck for workers of the Dutch West India Company.

BATTLING EUROPEANS AND INDIANS

From the time New Amsterdam was settled in the 1620s, the Dutch had French and English neighbors to their north and west. In 1638, the Swedes became their neighbors to the south. The colony of New Sweden was founded on the west bank of the Delaware River, on land that included modern-day Philadelphia. The leader of Sweden's first settlers was Peter Minuit, who had served the Dutch in New Netherland. By the early 1650s, the Swedes and Dutch were competing to control the fur trade in the region.

In 1654, Swedish troops took over Dutch Fort Kasimier in what is now New Castle, Delaware. Stuyvesant responded the next year by leading seven

The "Peach War"

WHILE STUYVESANT WAS BAT-tling the Swedes in 1655, Native Americans attacked settlers in New Amsterdam. Historians once called this strike on Manhattan the Peach War. Supposedly, the war started after a settler killed an Indian who had tried to steal peaches from his orchard. Russell Shorto offers another view of the attack in his 2004 book, *The Island at the Center of the World*. The attackers were led by Susquehannock Indians. The Indians had a trading relationship with the settlers of New Sweden. The Susquehannock were upset that the Dutch had gained control of the Swedes' land along the Delaware River. In effect, the Susquehannock were trying to help their allies, the Swedes. That help, however, was not enough to prevent the Dutch takeover of New Sweden.

ships and more than 600 troops to take it back. The Swedes were outnumbered, and they quickly surrendered the fort. With their victory, the Dutch took over New Sweden.

TROUBLES WITH THE ENGLISH

Despite their success against New Sweden, the Dutch faced problems with their other neighbors. The English argued with the Dutch over the boundaries between New Netherland and New England. England had claimed the land that became New Netherland in 1495 but never set up a colony there. In 1650, Stuyvesant decided to avoid a boundary dispute with the English by agreeing to give them the eastern half of Long Island and part of what is now southwestern Connecticut.

In 1652, disagreements over trade led to a war in Europe between England and the Netherlands. The English didn't want Dutch ships trading in England's colonial ports. The Dutch refused to give up their profitable trade. The war lasted from 1652 to 1654 and was fought mostly at sea. The Dutch finally agreed to end their trade in English ports. Relations between England and the Netherlands remained shaky. Starting in 1663, Dutch and English competition over the slave trade in Africa led to another war between the two nations.

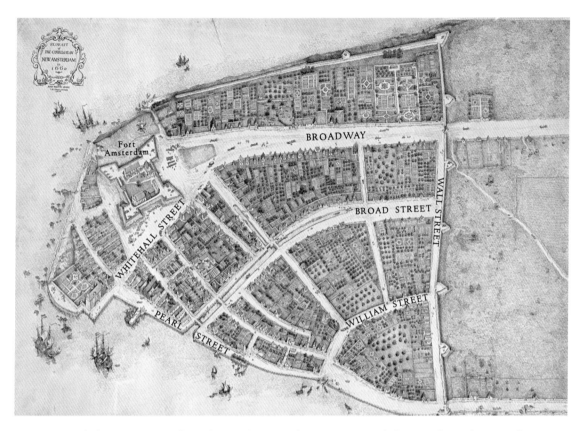

English street names have been added to this 1660 map of the Dutch settlement of
New Amsterdam. At the time, there were about 300 homes in the city. Dutch farms
called *bouweries* stretch beyond its northern limits, marked by Wall Street.

FROM NEW NETHERLAND
TO NEW YORK

After taking Dutch trading forts in Africa, England's King
Charles II decided to end the Dutch presence in North
America. In March 1664, Charles gave his brother James,
the Duke of York, land that included New Netherland.
James put together a fleet of four ships. Sailing under the

command of Colonel Richard Nicolls, the ships reached New Amsterdam in August. A message from Nicolls to Stuyvesant said, *"In his Majesty's Name I do demand the town, situate[d] upon the island commonly known as name of Manhattan."* Nicolls told the governor he would attack if the Dutch didn't surrender. If the colonists gave up, Nicolls promised to treat them well. Stuyvesant agreed to turn over New Amsterdam and the rest of New Netherland to the English. James soon renamed his new colony New York, and New Amsterdam became known as New York City.

Citizens of New Amsterdam watch as Peter Stuyvesant leads the Dutch Army out of the walled city and the English wait to take over after their victory in 1664.

The land Charles II gave his brother stretched between the Delaware and Connecticut Rivers. It also included part of Maine (which, at the time, was part of Massachusetts) and several islands off Massachusetts. James soon gave some of the land to friends and gave up control of other parts that were hard to defend. The heart of his colony was the land that later became the state of New York. The prize was the growing city at the tip of Manhattan Island. Richard Nicolls, who became the first English governor of New York, called New York City *"the best of all his Majesty's towns in America."* He saw its value as a trading port and center for business.

New York was unlike any other British colony on the mainland of North America. It was the only one not founded by English settlers. Its residents came from a large number of European countries. It was also the only colony controlled by a relative of the king. Yet the Duke of York never visited this land, choosing to have other people run it for him.

Under the terms of surrender, the States General of the Netherlands and the Dutch West India Company kept all the property they owned. Residents of any nationality were allowed to stay and keep their land and businesses. Freedom of religion enjoyed under the Dutch remained. In exchange, the residents of New York were asked to pledge their loyalty to the English king. As a result, Dutch influence remained strong for decades. ✽

CHAPTER FOUR

Colonial Life of the Dutch

THE COLONY THE ENGLISH *take over from the Dutch remains diverse, with a population that includes people from many European nations and African slaves.*

 efore 1664, the policies of the Dutch West India Company shaped who came to New Netherland. The first settlers, the Walloons, came as whole families. They were joined by single men who worked for the company as clerks, sailors, soldiers, fur traders, and craftsmen. Settlers came from England, Norway, Denmark, and several German states as well. The newcomers also included enslaved Africans. The first slaves arrived in New Amsterdam in 1626.

OPPOSITE: The Dutch had built a thriving slave trade in New Netherland by the early 1620s. Here traders in New Amsterdam take inventory of a new shipment of Africans.

This copper engraving shows the key ingredients to New Amsterdam's success: rich farmland (symbolized by the woman's basket of produce) and a thriving merchant class (symbolized by the well-dressed Dutchman), both of which relied on slave labor (shown in background on the left).

IN AND AROUND NEW AMSTERDAM

Besides raising their own food, farm families in and around Manhattan made many of their own goods, such as soap, candles, and yarn for clothing. Some of these workers and farmers also made extra money trapping animals for their fur. By 1640, this trapping was illegal, since the Dutch West India Company had a monopoly on the fur trade.

monopoly—exclusive control by one group of the production or sale of an item or service

New Amsterdam's growth as a business center began after 1640, when the Dutch West India Company gave up its monopoly on the fur trade. It wanted to encourage more settlers to come to the colony and opening up the fur trade was an incentive for many.

Merchants in the Netherlands invested money to transport goods back and forth across the Atlantic. In New Amsterdam, more stores soon appeared. Tailors, bakers, beer brewers, and tavern owners saw they could make money selling goods to the new immigrants and sailors visiting the city. People also invested in trading ships. The traders received part of the profit from the voyages, based on how much they invested. The ships carried timber as well as furs to Europe. On the trip back to New Amsterdam, they carried fine cloth, wine, manufactured goods, and other items not available in North America.

THE NORTHERN VILLAGE

THE DUTCH SETTLERS ON MANHATTAN REMAINED NEAR THE southern tip of the island for many years. In 1658, however, Peter Stuyvesant decided to start a farming community farther north on the island. The settlement, called Niuew Haarlem, would help defend the main community around Fort Amsterdam to the south. Today, Harlem is still the name of a well-known neighborhood in Manhattan. It has long been home to a vibrant African-American community.

An IMPORTANT JOB

ONE OF THE MOST IMPORTANT jobs in Beverwijck and the rest of New Netherland was brewing beer. Water was often not clean enough to drink, so the Dutch drank beer with every meal. Children drank what was called small beer, which had less alcohol than other beers. Adults drank special, expensive beers at holiday celebrations, weddings, and other important events. Dutch brewers were some of the Netherlands' wealthiest merchants. Kiliaen van Rensselaer proposed starting a brewery on his lands *"as soon as there is a supply of grain on hand"* so he could *"provide [beer to] all of New Netherland."*

LIFE IN THE NORTH

Besides New Amsterdam, the only other major Dutch settlement in New Netherland was near Fort Orange. First Rensselaerwijck and then Beverwijck were the centers of the fur trade for the colony. With the founding of Beverwijck, the farming community around Fort Orange developed into a town. Just five years after it was founded, Beverwijck had about 120 houses. Like New Amsterdam, it also attracted people from different ethnic and racial backgrounds.

FAMILY LIFE

In the colonial Dutch family, the father ran the farm or whatever business he owned. Dutch women of the 17th century had more rights than most other women in

Europe and North America. In both the Netherlands and New Netherland, women could own property, make contracts, and run a business. A wife's main role, however, was taking care of the family home and raising children. Under Dutch law, parents were supposed to take care of their children until they reached 25. Part of the parents' duty was making sure the children learned the basics of reading and writing as well as the skills to hold a job. Parents with enough money could pay to send their children to private grammar schools. New Amsterdam had a school as early as 1638.

A Dutch family gathers around the hearth in their home in colonial New York. The ceramic tiles around the fireplace were a popular decorative addition in the homes of those who could afford them.

SLAVES AND SERVANTS

Many of the young, single farmworkers who came to New Netherland were indentured servants. Before leaving the Netherlands, they signed an indenture, or contract, with a businessman who promised to pay for their trip across the Atlantic. In exchange, they worked for that person for a certain number of years, usually six. After their term of indenture was up, servants were free to go out on their own.

Slaves were also part of the workforce in New Netherland. By the time of the English takeover in 1664, there were about 400 African Americans in New Amsterdam. Most of them were slaves.

Slaves in New Netherland, as elsewhere, lacked the basic freedom to live and work as they chose. They had been forced from their homes in Africa and taken in chains across the Atlantic Ocean. Most slaves worked for the Dutch West India Company, although a few private citizens also owned some. Occasionally slaves were freed by the person they worked for. Both free Africans and slaves in New Netherland had more rights than other Africans in North America. By law, masters were not supposed to mistreat slaves, and slaves could take whites to court. Free blacks could own property and take any job they could find. Some free African Americans even hired white indentured servants.

Early Free
African Americans

HISTORIANS OF NEW NETHERLAND ARE STILL TRANSLATING documents from Dutch into English. One of these, not yet published as of 2005, describes the legal rights of free Africans to own property. Peter Stuyvesant wrote that the Africans had *true and free ownership* of *property*, with *such privileges as all tracts of land [given to] the inhabitants [of this] province*. The Dutch West India Company set aside land for some of the slaves it freed. The land was in a part of Manhattan now called Greenwich Village.

RELIGIOUS LIFE

By Dutch law, the people in the Netherlands and its colonies could belong to any religion they chose. But the Dutch Reformed Church, based on the Protestant faith, was the official Dutch church. Those settlers who were not Dutch brought with them a wide variety of religions. Natives of Denmark, Sweden, and Norway tended to be Lutheran, another Protestant faith. Germans belonged to a variety of Protestant faiths including Lutheran, although some were Roman Catholic. Many English Protestants were Puritan and, later, Anglican. Colonists with Spanish or Portuguese roots tended to be Catholic.

The first Jews in the colony reached New Amsterdam in 1654. They came from a Dutch colony in Brazil that had been captured by Portugal. Peter Stuyvesant, like many Christians of the day, disliked Jews. He believed that their religion was inferior to Christianity. The governor tried to keep the Jewish settlers out of the colony. The Dutch West India Company, however, forced him to accept them because many Jews had invested in the company. New Amsterdam's Jewish community grew steadily. Even though they could not worship in public, they had more legal rights in New Netherland than in any other North American colony.

CULTURE AND LEISURE

The settlers of New Netherland did not have much free time for arts and recreation. Few people owned any books besides the Bible. Young children might jump rope or fly kites, and the Dutch brought ice-skating with them from their homeland. For

Ice-skating, a popular sport in the Netherlands, was introduced by the Dutch to the American colonies.

adult men, such activities as cards and dice were popular, even if looked down on by the Dutch Reformed Church. Such activities, ministers thought, took people's attention away from God.

The Dutch influence lasted long after New Netherland became New York. For example, the Dutch brought their style of housing with them to North America. Their homes usually had frames in the shape of an H and were built out of wood, brick, or stone, depending on what was available. Roofs were often steep; later Dutch houses had gambrel roofs. Today, some houses with gambrel roofs are called Dutch colonials.

gambrel—a type of roof that has two slopes on each side, with the lower slope being the steeper of the two

The Dutch also brought with them the story of Sinter Klaus, a religious man who gave gifts to poor people. Sinter Klaus was the Dutch name for Saint Nicholas, who lived almost 2,000 years ago. In English, Sinter Klaus became Santa Claus, who is also sometimes known as Saint Nick. ✳

CHAPTER FIVE

An English Colony

Trouble sometimes erupts as the English try to govern. For a time, the Netherlands regains control of New York. Later, a Dutch resident leads a rebellion against the English.

 hen England took over New York in 1664, the colony had a population of about 6,000 people, much smaller than other British colonies such as Virginia and Massachusetts. The English protected the rights of the existing citizens, and in general, local governments still ran their own affairs, as they had under Dutch rule. The takeover by the English had not been violent, and the citizens were guaranteed, by the terms of the surrender,

OPPOSITE: New Amsterdam's Stadhuys (City Hall), which was first built as a tavern, occupied a prominent position along the waterfront. It later housed refugees fleeing from Indian attacks during Kieft's governorship.

ongoing religious tolerance. In addition, they were taxed equally by the British government and granted the same civil rights as British subjects, including trial by jury.

Adrien van der Donck

One feature of Dutch government in New Netherland was a position called the *schout*. This person served as the lawyer for the government, arguing its side in legal battles. The *schout* became known as the district, or prosecuting, attorney. Government lawyers with this title still exist today, bringing charges against accused criminals and arguing for their conviction. One of the first Dutch *schouts* was Adrien van der Donck. He argued that residents of New Netherland deserved the same rights as Dutch citizens in the Netherlands. In recent years, some historians have called Van der Donck one of the first Americans to demand democracy as a right everyone should enjoy.

The English did, however, institute some changes. In 1665, Nicolls—who had become governor—passed a series of laws that affected residents of Long Island and the region of Westchester, north of Manhattan. Under his so-called

Netherland would be too difficult. The colony was sur-
rounded by English colonies and would be hard to defend.
In November, the Dutch gave New Netherland back to
England, who named it New York again.

MORE CHANGES IN NEW YORK

The brief loss of New York to the Dutch wasn't the
colony's only problem. Between 1665 and 1682, residents
sometimes protested English policies. Taxes were a major
concern, and residents also wanted an elected lawmaking
assembly for the colony. One official wrote that the colony
was *"in the greatest confusion and disorder possible."* In 1683, the
Duke of York sent Thomas Dongan to New York to serve as
governor. He told Dongan to set up an elected assembly for
the colony that would meet in New York City.

New York's first Assembly was supposed to work with
the governor and his advisers to create laws and raise taxes.
Male freeholders in various towns elected a total of 17
members to the Assembly. Almost half of
them were Dutch. One of the Assembly's
first acts was writing a Charter of
Liberties and Privileges. This document spelled out certain
rights for the colonists. These included the right to follow
any religious faith and to face a jury if charged with a
crime. The governor and the duke approved the charter,

freeholders—colonists
who own their own land

and they also had final approval of any laws passed by the Assembly. With the charter and the Assembly, the residents of New York had more input in their government than ever before. But the central government—the governor, the council, and the king—still had the last word.

In 1685, King Charles II died, and his brother became King James II of England. New York was now called a royal colony under the direct control of the king. King James changed his mind about some of the powers he had granted New Yorkers and their Assembly when he was still a duke. The power to tax went back to the governor and his council, and the Assembly was shut down. In 1688, New York became part of a larger colonial unit known as the Dominion of New England. It included New Jersey, Massachusetts (including the Province of Maine), New Hampshire, Connecticut, and Rhode Island. The dominion's governor, based in Boston, was Sir Edmund Andros. He had served as governor of New York from 1684–1681.

Soon after New York became part of this enlarged New England, political trouble gripped England. James II was a Roman Catholic. Parliament was controlled by Protestants. James broke English law by giving Catholics important positions in the government. England was soon on the edge of civil war.

Parliament—
the branch of the
British government
that makes laws

In November 1688, Protestants forced King James from power. The new King and Queen, William and Mary, declared that no future king could disobey Parliament. The English called this their "Glorious Revolution" because they had reformed their government without spilling a drop of blood.

LEISLER'S REBELLION

During the Glorious Revolution, Massachusetts residents rebelled against Andros and forced him from power. In New York, the political changes led to chaos. In May 1689, the militia (local soldiers who volunteered to fight) seized Fort James, as Catholic officials loyal to King James fled the colony. A few weeks later, Jacob Leisler, a wealthy German-born Protestant merchant in New York City who had military ranking, took over the leadership of the fort. Thanks to his military experience, Leisler emerged as the head of the New York government. He led the people to believe that he was taking control of New York in order to secure it

In the spring of 1689, people in Boston, capital of the Dominion of New England, heard the news that James II was no longer king of England. They took the opportunity to overthrow the very unpopular Governor Andros. In New York, this paved the way for Jacob Leisler to come to power.

for William and Mary. In February 1690, Leisler called for a new Assembly to meet.

After Jacob Leisler announced that he was taking control of the government of New York, he knew he would need the support of the local militia. Here troops line up to sign a pledge of allegiance to him.

Leisler and his backers, who were mostly Dutch, were called Leislerians. Many of Leisler's supporters were laborers and artisans who resented the wealthier English who held most of the political power. Leisler wanted to redistribute some of the colony's wealth to the poor and form a government that would give more members of the working class a vote in what laws were passed. Leisler's opponents, the Anti-Leislerians, included the English and French residents who had come to the colony, and some Dutch. They resented Leisler's attempt to take power away from the wealthy merchants and aristocrats who held political power in the colony. Nicholas Bayard was one of the Dutch residents who opposed Leisler. He called the governor and his supporters *"a parcel of ignorant and innocent people."* Bayard and other Anti-Leislerians were sometimes thrown in jail even though they had committed no crime. After some of them tried to kill Leisler, even more of his political enemies were put behind bars so they would not try to weaken his rule.

In March 1691, Henry Sloughter arrived in New York. He was William and Mary's choice for the new governor. The King and Queen wanted someone less controversial running the colony in order to reclaim and insure English control. Leisler at first refused to give up his authority over the colony, as Sloughter demanded. Leisler finally realized he did not have the military strength to defy the English. After giving up power, he was arrested for murder and betraying the government. Leisler and his top aide were found guilty and executed.

CHAPTER SIX

A Century of Turmoil

New Yorkers face conflicts *with the French and Indians, while their politicians split into two major groups and battle to control the colony.*

 or decades, many historians saw Leisler's Rebellion as the last Dutch attempt to control New York. But the Dutch still held many political offices in New York City until 1730, and they played a role in the colony's government as well. Albany was almost two separate towns. Distinct populations of English and Dutch divided the city, and Dutch was widely spoken there through the 1750s. The Dutch continued to play an important economic role as merchants, shopkeepers, and artisans.

OPPOSITE: The Mohawk River linked New York's western frontier with Schenectady and Albany. By providing an easy way to transport furs and other trade goods, it contributed to the economic development of the region.

The English governors of New York during the 1690s and after had two main concerns. They wanted to strengthen the colonial economy and to protect the colony from invasion by other European powers and Indian alliances. The economy began to grow in the 18th century, thanks to the trade of flour, wheat, iron, and other goods. Defense on the frontier remained an issue much longer.

EUROPEAN CONFLICT IN NORTH AMERICA

In what became known as King William's War, the French and their Indian allies attacked the village of Schenectady in 1690, killing many of its people and burning most of the buildings. Some residents, many wearing only their nightclothes, managed to flee the city and find safety in Albany.

Tensions between England and France became heated in the early 1700s as both nations struggled for control of the fur trade in North America. An attack in 1690 on the predominantly Dutch inhabited town of Schenectady, north and west of Albany, was part of what the English called King William's War. During this war, the French battled both the English and their Iroquois allies. New York and other British colonies sent soldiers into Canada to attack the French, but their invasion failed. Finally, in 1697, France and England signed a peace treaty that ended King William's War.

Queen Anne's War broke out just five years later. It was fought mostly in New England. Once again, disputes over the fur trade between England and France fueled the war. At first, France convinced the Iroquois of New York to remain neutral, and little fighting took place in the colony. Twice, however, New York recruited several hundred men to take part in attacks on Canada. In 1709, New York leaders also convinced most of the Iroquois to end their neutrality and fight for England against France. But even with Indian help, the land invasions of Canada failed.

Queen Anne's War ended in 1713. The English forced France to give up some of its land in Canada, including Nova Scotia and Newfoundland. In the years that followed, the English built the first of several forts in northern New York. They were meant to protect the Iroquois from French attack and boost the English fur trade with the Indians. One of the most important forts was Fort Oswego, on the shores of Lake Ontario. Many Indians brought their furs there, reducing Albany's importance as a fur-trading center.

PROFILE

Peter Schuyler

During Queen Anne's War, Peter Schuyler was a key military figure in New York. He was born in Beverwijck (Albany), where his father was a successful Dutch fur trader and where Peter also did well in that business. The younger Schuyler learned the language of the Iroquois and often took part in meetings with them. He hoped to improve relations with the Indians and get their aid against the French. In 1709, Schuyler led the Indians who agreed to fight for the English. The next year, Schuyler destroyed a small fort the French had built within an Iroquois village. He told the Indians *that the French ought not to be permitted among them on any account whatsoever.*

NEW YORK POLITICS

As fighting with the French continued, New York went through a period of political uncertainty. In 1710, Robert Hunter became the governor. Serving for the next ten years, he struggled with the Assembly over taxes.

New York's political leaders were usually split into two groups. Wealthy landowners wanted leaders and government policies that protected them. They opposed taxes that were based on how much property a person owned. Most of the landed New Yorkers lived along the Hudson River, between New York City and Albany.

Opposing the landed interest was the merchant interest. This included men who had started their careers in the fur trade and then expanded into trading and shipping other goods. In general, merchants wanted lower duties on the goods they bought overseas and then resold in the colony. They opposed any limits on their freedom to trade where they wanted.

duties—taxes placed on goods brought into a colony or country

STRUGGLES FOR POWER

During Hunter's term as governor, he was friendly with the landed interest, whose members usually controlled the Assembly. They kept duties high. The leaders of the landed interest told the merchants that those *"who received an advantage by our trade, [should] contribute their [share] to the support"* of the colony. In 1720, William Burnet replaced Hunter as governor. He, like Hunter, also favored the landed interest over the merchants. He removed several merchants who served on the Council, as the governor's group of advisers was called. Burnet and his allies also restricted foreign trade, which almost forced some merchants to go out of business or to risk arrest by trading illegally.

Burnet left New York in 1727 to become governor of Massachusetts, but the struggle between the landed and merchant interests continued. The two sides began writing pamphlets to make fun of each other and to try to win support from voters.

pamphlets—booklets written on one particular subject

THE ZENGER TRIAL

The battle between New York's two parties for political power led to one of the most famous court cases in American history. In the middle of the political squabble was the German-born printer John Peter Zenger. In 1733, Zenger agreed to print a newspaper started by enemies of Governor William Cosby, who had arrived in New York the previous year. Zenger's articles criticized the governor, warning that "SLAVERY *is likely to be [placed] on*" the colonists because Cosby was depriving them of their lawful rights by excluding certain groups of people from voting in elections. Cosby was greedy, and he tried to change the government without the Assembly's approval.

In 1735, Cosby arrested Zenger for seditious libel. This meant Zenger had printed articles that the governor thought might lead to social unrest or weaken public support for the government. Under British law, a person found guilty of seditious libel went to jail. Up until this time, people charged with this crime couldn't avoid punishment even if they proved that what they wrote was true. If the

seditious libel— a crime involving the printing of words that might lead to social unrest, hurt the government's reputation, or weaken public support for rulers

governor was able to make the case that Zenger's words had caused trouble in the colony, then Zenger would be found guilty, despite whatever wrongdoing had been committed by the governor.

Zenger's lawyer was Andrew Hamilton. He argued that truth should be a defense against seditious libel. The jury, which disliked Cosby, agreed. Since what Zenger printed was true, the jury said, he should go free. People saw the value of having a truly free press, and more lawyers began to argue a defense for libel based on truth.

WORDS *for* FREEDOM

IN THE ZENGER TRIAL, ANDREW HAMILTON, A WELL-KNOWN Philadelphia lawyer, talked about some of the rights of New Yorkers that were in danger. He said,

It is not the cause of one poor printer . . . which you are now trying. No! It may in its consequence affect every free man that lives under a British government on the main of America. It is the best cause. It is the cause of liberty . . . nature and the laws of our country have given us a right to liberty of both exposing and opposing arbitrary power . . . by speaking and writing the truth.

THE FRENCH AND INDIAN WAR

After several decades of peaceful relations, the 1740s saw France and Great Britain fighting again in North America. In 1754, a young officer from Virginia named George Washington led American militia against French and Indian forces in the valley of the Ohio River. France's allies included the Chippewa, Ottawa, and Shawnee Indians. These battles marked the start of what Americans later called the French and Indian War.

English settlers are massacred by Indians allied with the French at Fort William Henry on Lake George, New York, in 1757.

For the next several years, the British and French battled in New York near Lakes George, Champlain, and Ontario. The victories were divided, but the English Army persevered. If the British could gain control of these areas, the French would effectively be cut off from their strongholds in Montreal and Quebec in New France. By the end of 1760, the tide had turned in favor of the British. The fighting in North America was over and the British had won. France and Great Britain signed the Treaty of Paris three years later, officially ending the French and Indian War and French rule on the continent of North America. ✽

"Brave Old Hendrick" was a great Mohawk chief who allied his tribe with the British during the French and Indian War. This Indian warrior, shown here in English clothing, was killed in battle on September 8, 1755, near Lake George, New York.

Sir   New york 3.ᵗ March 1762.

You are hereby notified of a Meeting of the Hand-in-Hand Fire Company at the House of Mʳ Crawley, at the City Arms on Thursday next at Seven o'Clock in the Evening

To The Rᵗ Honᵇˡᵉ., The Earl of Sterling.

Isaac Roosevelt Clerk

CHAPTER SEVEN

A Growing Colony

NEW YORK CITY AND ALBANY *remain the centers of commerce as the colony grows and prospers.*

 ew York was a place of great change in the 18th century. New York City continued to grow as a center of trade. By 1743, the population reached 11,000. At that time, New York was the third-largest city in British North America, behind Boston and Philadelphia. By 1750, the entire colony of New York had 80,000 people, and that number would double during the next 20 years.

OPPOSITE: New York City suffered many fires during colonial times. This invitation for a meeting of the Hand-in-Hand Fire Company shows the standard means of fighting fires at the time: colonists man a bucket brigade that passes water from a pump to the fire engine, while others carry ladders to rescue people from burning buildings.

A Variety of People

The Anglican Church was the official church of Great Britain, but the policy of religious tolerance that went back to the days of the Dutch West India Company remained in place. Protestants of all kinds worshipped freely in New York. Some of the Protestants who came to New York were Huguenots. These French Protestants had been forced to flee their homeland in 1685. About 2,000 crossed the Atlantic Ocean and settled in British colonies, including New York. They made up one of the larger ethnic groups in New York City. Many Huguenots were merchants, with the DeLancey family being the most successful.

Lasting Contribution

MANY OF THE HUGUENOTS settled in New Paltz, north of New York City. At first they lived in small wooden houses, but soon they built larger homes out of stone. Recent research by archaeologists shows that the first of these stone houses appeared in the early 1680s. Today, one road in New Paltz, called Huguenot Street, has six surviving stone houses. It is the oldest street in America that still has some of its original homes standing. These houses are open to the public and display furniture and other items used by their colonial residents.

OPPOSITE: This 1677 agreement between the Esopus and the settlers of New Paltz is signed by Governor Andros and the town's Huguenot inhabitants. The markings made by the Indians appear at the bottom right.

I do allow of the within bargaine, and shall
graunt Patents for ye same, when payments
made accordingly before mee or Magistrates
of Esopus.

ANDROS.

Wij ondergeschreven... gevonden...
Landt... aen Louris du Prooij's...
... Van Gal... ten volle voldaen
te sijn volgens accordt...
... Landt met...
... gedaen met...
van... regt in...
alle... hebben bij...
Naktros...
... onderteeckent... 15 September
1637 tot Arolj

Fairly large numbers of Scottish immigrants began to arrive in New York during the 18th century. Some came directly from Scotland, while others—a group known as the Scots-Irish—came from Ireland, where they had moved earlier. These immigrants settled in New York City and farther north along the Hudson River. Robert Livingston, a leader of the landed interest in New York politics, was of Scottish descent. So was Cadwallader Colden, a noted scholar and politician. Most Scots and Scots-Irish belonged to the Presbyterian Church.

Parishioners make their way home after church in Sleepy Hollow, New York. Some of the old Dutch churches of the colonial era still stand in this village along the Hudson River not far from New York City.

In 1709, Governor Robert Hunter arranged for a group of Germans who had lost their jobs and homes to a great war in Europe to settle in New York. These Germans came from a region called the Palatinate, in western Germany, and were called Palatines. About 2,000 of these immigrants moved to towns along the Hudson River. A few Germans who came to the colony were Jewish. They settled in New York City, and by 1730 the Jewish community there numbered 75 families. The first synagogue in North America was erected in New York later that year. Other German immigrants were Roman Catholic. Under British rule, they couldn't worship in public.

CITY LIFE

Since New York's founding, its residents had focused on trade and making money. New York City and Albany remained the colony's main cities, though New York City was clearly the

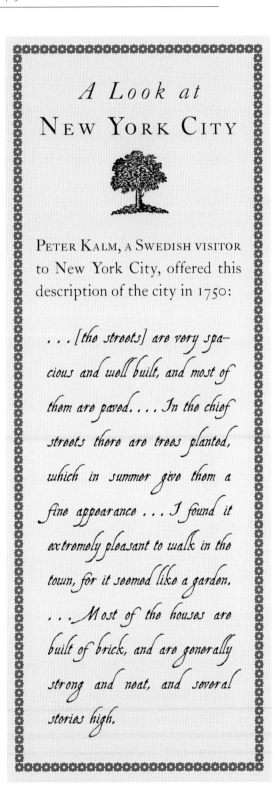

A Look at
NEW YORK CITY

PETER KALM, A SWEDISH VISITOR to New York City, offered this description of the city in 1750:

. . . [the streets] are very spacious and well built, and most of them are paved. . . . In the chief streets there are trees planted, which in summer give them a fine appearance . . . I found it extremely pleasant to walk in the town, for it seemed like a garden. . . . Most of the houses are built of brick, and are generally strong and neat, and several stories high.

more important of the two. It was the major port for shipping goods overseas and to other North American colonies.
Some of the most important products were wheat, flour,
timber, meat, and pelts. New York City also had mills that
refined raw sugar imported from the West Indies into sugar
used in food. Many of the goods that moved through New
York City went to Great Britain and British and Dutch
colonies in the West Indies.

The growth of trade in New York City led to the rise
of banks, insurance companies, attorneys and other businesses. A variety of merchants also served the needs of the
city's population. These included dressmakers, tavern
keepers, barbers, and shoemakers. The city also still had
farms, and pigs sometimes ran wild through the streets.

Just as in modern cities, New York City had great
extremes of wealth and poverty. Rich women paraded
through the streets in fine dresses, and their husbands
bought silver and other expensive items from overseas for
their homes. Poor adults and children begged in the streets
for money, and the city spent more to try to help these
people than on any other single issue.

The greatest number of New York City's residents
were hardworking farmers and artisans. Some artisans
both farmed and practiced their crafts.
Artisans relied on apprentices for help,
though some also hired workers. A newspaper ad from 1726 said, *"Three or four good*

apprentices—young
people bound by legal
agreement to work in
return for instruction in
a specific trade

hands that understand the burning of charcoal, may have employ-
ment and good wages for a year, or longer."

City women—as well as farm women—still centered
their lives on home and family. British laws, however, gave
women fewer rights than they had under the Dutch. Under
British rule, fewer women were able to go into business,
although widows were allowed to continue to run their
husbands' businesses. In 1733, a group of these female merchants complained to the government: "We . . . pay our taxes . . .
and as we in some measure contribute to the support of government, we
ought to be entitled to some of the [benefits] of it." The government
ignored their plea.

BATTLE OVER LAND

ALONG THE HUDSON RIVER, THE SHORTAGE OF LAND
available for sale finally led to violence. In 1766, frustrated
tenants—sometimes as many as 2,000 strong—
frequently banded together to demand land for themselves. Landowners and local officials called in sheriffs
and British soldiers to battle the protesters. In one case,
the soldiers attacked the tenants' homes. One observer
noted that "some [were] demolished, some robbed . . . and
others of them [were] enveloped in flames of fire." Local
officials were finally able to end the riots a few years after
they had begun.

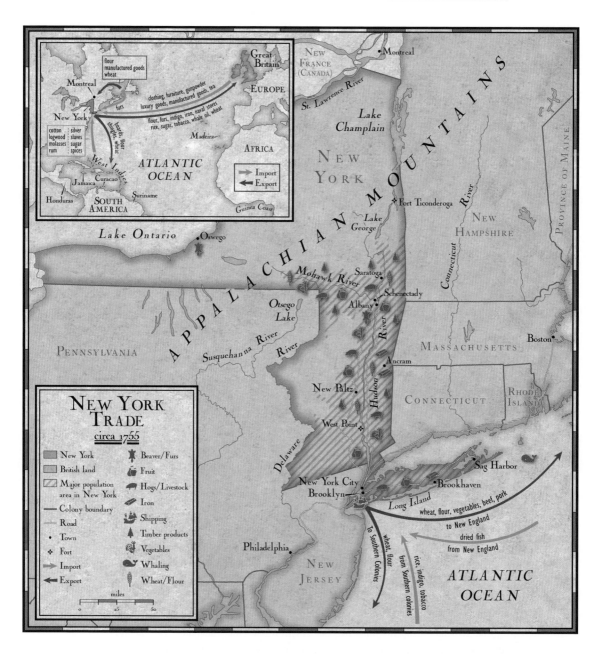

By 1750, New York was fast becoming the primary trading center in colonial America. From the valleys of the Hudson and Mohawk Rivers came most of its exports: wheat, livestock, naval stores (pitch, turpentine, and tar), and other agricultural products. Britain and areas in and around the West Indies, including Dutch-controlled Curaçao and Suriname, were its chief trading partners. New York City, with its excellent harbor, was developing into a shipping center. This, in turn, gave rise to banking, insurance, brokerage houses and other commercial enterprises associated with present-day New York.

COUNTRY LIFE

Along the Hudson River and on Long Island, wealthy land-owners dominated the economy. One person or family some-times owned hundreds of thousands of acres—more than they could afford to farm. Yet the landowners were not willing to sell the land. Instead, they rented small plots to tenant farmers.

The homes of the wealthy landowners were large and filled with fine furniture. The wealthy were likely to be well educated, though a large number of common people learned the basics of reading and writing.

Steven Van Rensselaer, who was a direct descendant of New Netherland's first patroon, Kiliaen Van Rensselaer, inherited vast amounts of land along the Hudson near Albany. More than 3,000 tenant farmers lived and worked on his land.

Farming was not the only way to make a living outside of the cities. Whaling boats based on Long Island sailed into the Atlantic to hunt these sea mammals. Their blubber was a valuable source of oil, which was used for lighting and manufacturing soap, wool, and leather. Whaling also led to a demand for wooden barrels to store whale oil, creating another source of jobs. During the 18th century, New York also had a small iron industry. Iron ore mined in the colony was turned into metal at sites called forges. The forges were located near rivers, so the rushing water could be used to power equipment. One early iron forge was at Brookhaven, on Long Island, and another at Ancram, now Copake, in the Catskill mountains of New York.

The slave market at the foot of Wall Street in New York City around 1730

THE INCREASING
IMPORTANCE OF SLAVERY

Under English rule, slavery became more common in New York, and especially in New York City. In 1703, there were more than 2,000 blacks in the colony, and approximately 700 of them were slaves. A census in 1771 showed almost

20,000 African Americans in the colony—about 11 percent of the total population.

Most slaveowners who lived in New York owned only one or two slaves. Slaves often toiled in workshops or as domestic servants. Other slaves labored building the roads, houses, and forts of the New York colony, or clearing land and working on farms throughout the Hudson Valley.

UNCOVERING THE PAST

In 1991, U.S. government officials announced they had found a cemetery in New York City that was once used to bury slaves. Archaeologists soon began digging at this African Burial Ground to see what they could learn about slave life in colonial New York. One thing they have learned is that the slaves kept some of the burial practices they had used in Africa. Bodies were sometimes buried with personal items, such as jewelry. The teeth of some dead slaves had been filed into the shape of an hourglass. And the bodies were often buried with their heads pointing toward Africa.

The slave trade was an important source of income for some New Yorkers. Leading merchant families, including the Philipses, Van Cortlandts, and Livingstons, owned ships that carried slaves from Africa or the West Indies. New

York City had a slave market, where people came to buy and sell slaves. During the colonial era, the city was one of the major slave-trading centers in British North America.

SLAVE LIFE

As in other colonies, enslaved African Americans had little family life. Slaves didn't have many chances to meet with each other, making it hard for men and women to fall in love and marry. If two slaves did marry, they often lived with different masters. The greatest fear of slaves was being sold to an owner in another colony, far from their families. Slaves were property, and masters could sell them whenever they chose.

The legal system made life hard for blacks who had arrived in the colony as free men, or former slaves who had purchased their freedom. A white could claim that a free black was a slave, and it was up to the African American to prove she or he was free. Under English rule, the colony repealed the Dutch law that allowed freed slaves to own property.

repeal—to overturn or withdraw a law

The anger most slaves felt over having no freedom led some to rebel. New York City saw two bloody slave rebellions during colonial times. In 1712, a group of slaves managed to steal and hide several guns and other weapons. They then set fire to a building. When white citizens came to put out the fire, the rebels attacked them, killing nine

Violence Over Slavery

GOVERNOR ROBERT HUNTER sent a letter to British officials describing the slave rebellion of 1712. Here is some of what he wrote:

. . . they [the slaves] agreed to meet in the orchard of Mr. Crook in the middle of town, some provided with firearms, some with swords and others with knives and hatchets. . . . Upon the first notice . . . I ordered a detachment [of soldiers] from the fort under a proper officer to march against them, but the slaves made their retreat into the woods . . . by . . . strict searches in the town, we found all that put the [plan together].

people and wounding others. At least 18 slaves were found guilty and executed.

The 1712 uprising led to the enactment of strict laws against blacks. By 1740, the white population was becoming nervous about the growing number of blacks in the city, especially after learning about a slave revolt in South Carolina. There was also resentment among poor whites, who accused blacks of taking jobs away from them. A series of suspicious fires broke out in the spring of 1741. These led to the arrests and deaths of several blacks who were accused of plotting to burn down the city and kill the white population. Today, historians differ about whether the fires were part of a slave revolt or the work of white people who wanted to rid the city of its large African population. ✳

CHAPTER EIGHT

Revolutionary New York

DURING THE AMERICAN REVOLUTION, *many New Yorkers remain loyal to Great Britain, and several important battles are waged across the colony.*

he 1760s marked the beginning of a crucial period for colonial New York. With Great Britain's victory in the French and Indian War, King George III ordered a series of forts to be built in the west beyond the Appalachians. He wanted to keep peace between the Indians and the settlers who had been prohibited by proclamation in 1763 from establishing settlements on the Native lands in this region. The King meant for the forts to be a show of confidence to the Indians that he would

OPPOSITE: A fire that broke out in New York after the British took over the city destroyed hundreds of buildings but did not cause the British to leave. The city served as Britain's headquarters throughout the Revolutionary War.

enforce the new law and try to keep the peace. To pay for the forts, the British wanted to collect new taxes throughout the Colonies.

In 1764, Parliament passed the Sugar Act which placed a duty on the purchase of sugar. New York shippers carried sugarcane (raw sugar) and its by-product molasses from the West Indies to the Colonies, where it was used to make rum. Both shippers and rum makers feared losing money if they had to pay a tax on sugar. In October 1764, New York's Assembly protested the Sugar Act. The lawmakers argued that the tax on sugar would hurt local businesses, including taverns, merchants, and importers.

GROWING ANGER ON TWO SIDES

With the working class and merchants feeling their rights increasingly at risk, some New Yorkers turned to violence. When, in 1765, Parliament passed a law that taxed newspapers and legal documents, New Yorkers and other Americans quickly responded. People who opposed this Stamp Act took to the streets to protest. The leaders of the protest were known as Sons of Liberty, or Patriots. Cadwallader Colden, the lieutenant governor of New York who had strong ties to King George, later wrote that the Sons and other protesters *openly threatened to destroy every thing I had in both town and country.* In October, Patriot leaders from nine colonies met in New York City to voice their anger over the tax. The meeting was called the Stamp Act Congress. By this time, merchants in New York and other major American cities were boycotting, or refusing to buy, British goods. British merchants pressured Parliament to repeal the Stamp Act. Parliament agreed but said it still had the right to collect other taxes in the Colonies.

New Yorkers take to the streets to protest the Stamp Act, one of several laws passed by Parliament that would lead to revolution.

In 1767, Parliament passed a series of duties called the Townshend Acts. Taxes were collected on several goods brought into the Colonies, including tea. In 1770, Parliament repealed most of the duties, except for the tax

The "Battle" of GOLDEN HILL

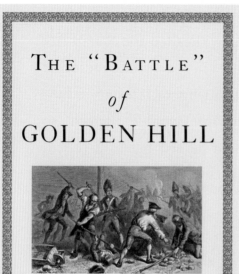

In the Boston Massacre of March 1770, a group of British soldiers killed five colonists who had been taunting them. Fewer know about fighting that took place two months earlier in New York City at a place called Golden Hill. British troops stationed in New York upset some residents when they pulled down a liberty pole. The pole had been set up as a meeting place for the Sons of Liberty. Residents armed with clubs fought with British soldiers, and several people were injured.

on tea. People across the Colonies promised to boycott British tea, or purchase only smuggled tea. In 1773, Britain tried to encourage Americans to buy British tea by lowering its price. But the tax remained in place, which angered many Patriots. In December 1773, New Yorkers learned that Boston Patriots had raided three ships that had cargoes of tea waiting to be brought ashore and taxed. The Patriots threw the tea into the harbor, an action soon known as the Boston Tea Party. Early in 1774, New Yorkers staged their own protest, throwing tea into New York harbor.

British officials reacted angrily to the Boston Tea Party. They passed new laws that the colonists called the Intolerable Acts. These laws limited freedom in the Colonies in many ways, including forcing colonists to house British soldiers at their own expense and closing the port of Boston until damages from the Boston Tea Party were paid to the British government. To protest the Intolerable Acts, the New York Assembly called for the American colonies to send delegates to a meeting to determine how to respond.

delegates—people chosen to represent larger groups

THE ROAD TO REVOLUTION

The meeting of colonial delegates held in Philadelphia in the fall of 1774 was called the First Continental Congress. Most of the representatives assumed that the disagreements with Great Britain could be resolved peacefully. That hope, however, ended in the spring when Massachusetts citizens in Lexington and the neighboring town of Concord exchanged shots with the British, marking the start of the American Revolution. After learning of the fighting, the New York Assembly agreed to send delegates to a Second Continental Congress. At the congress, the Colonies would decide how to work together to fight the British.

New Yorkers had mixed feelings about breaking ties with Great Britain. Many truly worried about losing rights they had enjoyed for years as British subjects. Merchants feared the end of trade with Great Britain and its West Indian colonies. A large number of New Yorkers were Loyalists—they remained loyal to King George and opposed the Revolution. New York had more Loyalists than any other northern colony. Many of them lived in and around New

York City and on Long Island. Albany and the counties around it tended to have more Patriots. The loudest calls for challenging the British came from the artisans and others who did not have much local political power. They hoped that the war would lead to changes within New York that would weaken the control of the wealthy over the colony.

BATTLES IN NEW YORK

In 1775, northern New York was the site of a key Patriot victory. In May, troops led by Benedict Arnold and Ethan Allen captured Fort Ticonderoga. Other major battles in New York took place the next year, in and around New York City. George Washington, the commander of the American troops, wanted to keep the city under Patriot control. Whoever held New York City controlled the mouth of the Hudson River as well as the most important harbor for moving troops and supplies into the northern colonies.

By March 1776, the Patriot army had forced the British out of Boston. Washington soon began marching his troops from Massachusetts to New York. The British had retreated to Nova Scotia, in what is now Canada to regroup and wait for reinforcements. They knew the importance of controlling New York City. In July 1776, the British landed 10,000 troops on Staten Island, and twice as many soon reached the city. By August, Washington had only about 10,000 men able to fight this large and well-trained force.

Before the battle for New York began, the Continental Congress made a major decision. On July 2, it voted for independence. Two days later, the delegates approved the Declaration of Independence. The 13 former colonies were now united as states in one nation—the United States. At the signing on August 2, four New Yorkers proudly added their signatures to this historic document: William Floyd, Philip Livingston, Francis Lewis, and Lewis Morris. A week after the signing, New York Patriots pulled down a statue of King George that stood on Bowling Green in New York City and melted it down to make bullets for Washington's Continental Army.

Patriots in New York City pull down the Statue of King George III to celebrate the signing of the Declaration of Independence.

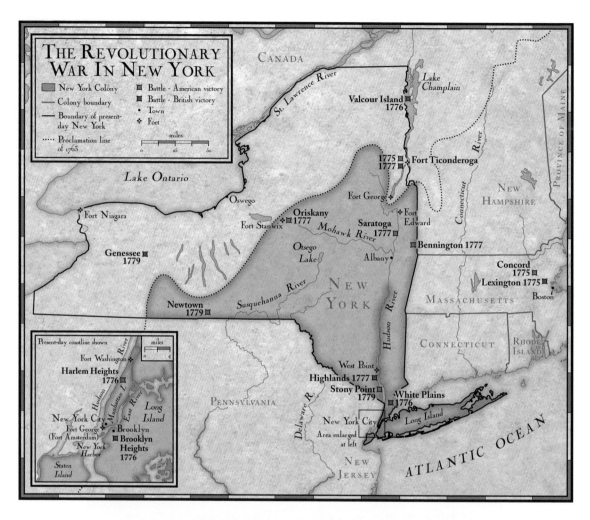

THE REVOLUTIONARY WAR IN NEW YORK

New York Colony
Colony boundary
Boundary of present-day New York
Proclamation line of 1763
Battle - American victory
Battle - British victory
Town
Fort

miles
0   25   50

CANADA

St. Lawrence River

Lake Champlain

Lake Ontario

Valcour Island 1776

Oswego

Fort Niagara

1775 1777 Fort Ticonderoga

Fort George

Oriskany 1777

Fort Stanwix

Mohawk River

Saratoga 1777

Fort Edward

Connecticut River

NEW HAMPSHIRE

PROVINCE OF MAINE

Bennington 1777

Genessee 1779

Otsego Lake

Albany

Concord 1775
Lexington 1775

NEW YORK

MASSACHUSETTS

Boston

Newtown 1779

Susquehanna River

Hudson River

CONNECTICUT

RHODE ISLAND

Present-day coastline shown
miles
0   4

Fort Washington

Harlem Heights 1776

Hudson River

East River

Manhattan I.

Long Island

New York City
Fort George (Fort Amsterdam)

Brooklyn

Brooklyn Heights 1776

New York Harbor

Staten Island

PENNSYLVANIA

Delaware R.

West Point

Highlands 1777

Stony Point 1779

White Plains 1776

New York City
Area enlarged at left

Long Island

ATLANTIC OCEAN

NEW JERSEY

New York was an important battleground during the American Revolution. The British victory at Brooklyn Heights in August 1776 paved the way for their takeover of New York City, which remained their headquarters throughout the war. Their efforts in the northern part of the colony were not so successful. Britain wanted to cut off New England from the rest of the colonies by gaining control of the Hudson River. The retaking of Fort Ticonderoga in July 1777 seemed a promising step toward this goal, but victory was short-lived. The Patriot triumph at Saratoga on October 17 was a major turning point in the war. Not only did it end Britain's advance along the Hudson, it also convinced France to enter the war as America's ally.

HARD-FOUGHT VICTORY

Before the battle for New York, Loyalists in New York City plotted to kill George Washington. They also had planned, as a Patriot later wrote, to *"murder all the staff officers, blow up the [warehouses], and secure the [roads] of the town."* The plotters included the mayor of New York and two of Washington's guards. None of this ever came to pass.

The Battle of Long Island, which pitted 20,000 British troops against 10,000 American soldiers, forced a retreat that eventually left New York City in British hands.

In August 1776, the British made their move in New York. They sent troops from Staten Island to Long Island, beginning a three-week-long battle for control of New York City. The Americans could not match the more powerful British forces. A frustrated Washington cried, *"Good God, what brave fellows I must this day lose!"* Washington pulled his troops out of the city in September. The British used the city as their headquarters for the rest of the war.

The Americans had better luck in northern New York, where Benedict Arnold forced the British to delay their advance down Lake Champlain for almost a year. In October 1777, American forces under Horatio Gates won a major victory at Saratoga, north of Albany. Upon hearing that the Americans had won an important battle, the French decided to join the war against the British.

During the American Revolution, both sides sought help from the six tribes of Native Americans that were now united under the Iroquois. The Oneida and Tuscarora aided the Americans, while the other four tribes backed the British. Mohawk chief Thayendenegea, better known as Joseph Brant, led the four tribes that fought for Great Britain. Joint Indian-British attacks on American towns led the Americans to counterattack in 1779. An American officer described how his men destroyed Indian crops and homes, *"leaving the towns in flames."* At the end of the war, the Iroquois lost most of their land to the Americans, as waves of settlers occupied land once held by these Indians.

In 1781, the last major battle of the Revolution was fought in Yorktown, Virginia. With aid from France, General Washington and his troops forced the British to surrender. The war officially ended in 1783, when British and American officials signed the Treaty of Paris.

Benedict Arnold

The most famous traitor of the war did some of his greatest and worst deeds in New York. In 1775, Benedict Arnold helped lead a surprise takeover of Fort Ticonderoga and fought bravely at Saratoga in 1777. But by 1780, he felt that U.S. leaders were not giving him the credit—or money—he deserved. He decided to help the British by giving them control of the most important fort on the Hudson River: West Point, which he commanded. If the British held the fort, they could prevent the Americans from bringing supplies from New England to New York and other states. The plot failed, and Arnold narrowly escaped capture.

Americans were outraged by Benedict Arnold's treasonous acts against the United States. This woodcut shows an effigy, or likeness, of the two-faced traitor sitting in front of a devil figure waiting to be burned.

BUILDING AN
INDEPENDENT NEW YORK

Even before the war was over, New York's
Patriots created the first constitution for
the state, approved in April 1777. The
new government had a legislature with
two parts, the Assembly and the Senate.
Voters, men who owned or rented prop-

constitution—a docu-
ment that outlines a
state or nation's form of
government and the
procedures for making
and enforcing laws

erty, elected the lawmakers and the governor. The governor, along with judges from the state supreme court,
could suggest changes to proposed laws, but the legislature
still had the final say.

The Articles of Confederation, created by the
Continental Congress during the Revolution, set up the
country's first national government. This document gave the
central U.S. government very little power. If the United
States was going to survive, it would need a more effective
form of government that was supported by all the states.

Alexander Hamilton, a New Yorker, was one of the
country's leaders who thought America needed a stronger
national government. In September 1787, delegates met at
the Constitutional Convention in Philadelphia to create the
U.S. Constitution, which is still the basic framework of
America's national government. New York sent three delegates to the convention: Alexander Hamilton, John Lansing,
and Robert Yates. Only Hamilton signed the Constitution,

as the others had left early. Hamilton and a New York lawyer named John Jay, along with James Madison, a delegate from Virginia, led the battle to convince all the states to ratify, or approve, the document. The three men published a series of articles that presented arguments supporting why the country needed a stronger national government. The articles are known as the *Federalist Papers*.

⊠⊠⊠⊠⊠⊠⊠⊠⊠   P R O F I L E   ⊠⊠⊠⊠⊠⊠⊠⊠⊠

John Jay

John Jay came from a wealthy New York family. He studied at King's College (now Columbia University) before becoming a successful lawyer. As the American Revolution approached, he hoped the Colonies would reach a peaceful settlement with Great Britain. Once the Americans declared independence, however, he strongly supported that cause. Jay helped write New York's constitution of 1777 and held several positions in the early governments of the United States. Along with John Adams and Benjamin Franklin, Jay helped negotiate the Treaty of Paris, which ended the Revolution in 1783. In 1789, he became the first chief justice of the U.S. Supreme Court, and he later served as governor of New York. In the *Federalist Papers*, Jay wrote that *"the prosperity of the people of America depend[s] on their continuing firmly united."*

The *Federalist Papers*

IN OCTOBER 1787, NEW YORK READERS SAW A LETTER IN A local newspaper signed by someone named Publius. The author said he planned to publish a series of articles explaining why Americans should support the new Constitution of the United States. Over the next few months, 84 more letters by Publius appeared in several New York papers. The articles were also published in a book that was read all over the country. Publius was the pen name used by Alexander Hamilton, James Madison, and John Jay as they wrote what are now called the *Federalist Papers*. Historians believe that Hamilton wrote 51 of the articles, Madison 26, and Jay 5. Madison and Hamilton worked together on another three. Today, the *Federalist Papers* is not just a historical document. Legal experts and lawmakers still read it to try to understand how the founders of the U.S. government wanted the country run.

In the first article, Hamilton wrote that the new national government would provide *"additional security . . . to the preservation of . . . liberty, and to property."* New Yorkers were deeply divided about accepting the Constitution. Many thought that the new government took away too much power from the states. Others were concerned that the poor and middle classes would be oppressed by the rich. But on July 26, 1788, New York became the eleventh state to ratify the

Constitution. The next year, George Washington was elected as America's first president. New York City served as the capital of the federal government. New Yorkers came out to cheer their new president and the government they had created. The days when a distant Dutch company ruled New Netherland were long gone. Thanks to its thriving port city at the mouth of the river Henry Hudson had explored almost 200 years before, New York was ready to become one of the most important states in the new nation.

George Washington is sworn in as the first President of the United States by Robert Livingston on the balcony of Federal Hall in New York City. Standing to Washington's left is John Adams, the first Vice President.

TIME LINE

1609 English captain Henry Hudson, sailing for the Netherlands, explores the river that will later be named for him. Frenchman Samuel de Champlain explores the region around a lake that will be named for him.

1614 Dutch officials use the name "New Netherland" for the first time. Dutch sailors build Fort Nassau.

1621 Dutch investors receive a charter to form the Dutch West India Company.

1624 The Dutch West India Company sends the first settlers to New Netherland.

1626 Peter Minuit buys Manhattan from the Munsee Indians and begins building a fort on the southern tip of the island. The first African slaves are brought to New Netherland.

1630 Kiliaen Van Rensselaer becomes a patroon, receiving land near Fort Orange (Albany).

1640 Governor Willem Kieft begins a series of wars with the Indians, which kills almost 1,000 Indians and destroys many Dutch farms.

1652 Governor Peter Stuyvesant takes control of land near Rensselaerwijck and creates the town of Beverwijck. The Dutch win control of all of Sweden's land in North America. New Netherland's first Jewish residents settle in New Amsterdam (New York City.)

1664 English naval forces capture New Amsterdam. Under English control, New Netherland is renamed New York; New Amsterdam becomes New York City; Beverwijck is called Albany.

1673 Dutch forces briefly recapture New York but soon give the colony back to the English.

1680s French Protestants called Huguenots begin settling in New York.

1683 New York's first Assembly makes laws for the colony.

1688 King James II adds New York to the Dominion of New England.

1689 Jacob Leisler seizes control of New York's government in what is later called Leisler's Rebellion.

1690 French soldiers from Canada join with Indians to attack Schenectady, a town northwest of Albany. More than 60 residents are killed.

1709 New Yorkers and some Iroquois battle the French and their Indian allies during Queen Anne's War.

1712 New York's first slave uprising takes place.

1720s New Yorkers build Fort Oswego, near the eastern end of Lake Ontario.

1735 Printer John Peter Zenger is found innocent of seditious libel.

1741 Blacks accused of trying to burn the city are arrested and executed.

1764 The New York Assembly protests the Sugar Act.

1765 Delegates from nine colonies meet in New York at the Stamp Act Congress. New York responds to the Intolerable Acts by urging delegates from each colony to meet in Philadelphia.

1775 The American Revolution begins in Massachusetts. In May, American troops capture Fort Ticonderoga in northern New York.

1776 The British land about 30,000 troops in New York. These forces battle Americans under the command of George Washington in and around New York City. The Americans are forced to retreat, leaving New York City under British control.

1777 New York lawmakers create the state's first constitution. American troops defeat the British at Saratoga. France decides to fight for the Americans.

1783 Great Britain and the United States sign a peace treaty that ends the American Revolution.

1787 Representing New York, Alexander Hamilton signs the U.S. Constitution. He and John Jay, along with Virginian James Madison, write the *Federalist Papers* defending the need for a strong central government.

1788 New York is the 11th state to ratify the U.S. Constitution.

1789 George Washington is sworn in as the first U.S. President in New York City.

RESOURCES

BOOKS

Barter, James. *Colonial New York*. San Diego: Lucent Press, 2004

Bullock, Steven C. *The American Revolution: A History in Documents*. New York: Oxford University Press, 2003.

Fischer, Laura. *Life in New Amsterdam*. Chicago: Heinemann Library, 2003.

Haugen, Brenda. *Alexander Hamilton: Founding Father and Statesman*. Minneapolis: Compass Point Books, 2005.

Jameson, J. Franklin. *Narratives of New Netherland, 1609–1664*. New York: Barnes and Noble, 1959.

Krizner, L. J. *Peter Stuyvesant: New Amsterdam and the Origins of New York*. New York: PowerKids Press, 2002.

* Shannon, Timothy J. *Indians at the Crossroads of Empire: The Albany Congress of 1754*. Ithaca, New York: Cornell University Press, 2002.

Sneve, Virginia Driving Hawk. *The Iroquois*. Mankato, Minnesota: Bridgestone Press, 2002.

Wood, Peter. *Strange New Land: African Americans, 1617–1776*. New York: Oxford University Press, 1996.

Worth, Richard. *Saratoga*. Philadelphia: Chelsea House Publishers, 2002.

* college-level source

WEB SITES

Colonial Albany Social History Project
http://www.nysm.nysed.gov/albany/welcome.html
Part of the New York State Museum, the Albany Project has biographies and pictures of important people in the history of colonial Albany, as well as a detailed history of life in the city.

Iroquois Indian Museum
http://www.iroquoismuseum.org/index.htm
The Web site for this museum has both historical and current information on the Six Nations.

Liberty! The American Revolution
http://www.pbs.org/ktca/liberty/index.html
This site is based on a television series and book of the same name, and it describes some of the battles that took place in New York.

Long Island—Our Story
http://www.newsday.com/community/guide/lihistory/
From the Long Island newspaper *Newsday*, a look at the history of Long Island. The site has sections on Long Island's Indians, its colonial history, and its role during the American Revolution.

The New York Constitution
http://www.yale.edu.lawweb/avalon/states/ny01.htm
A copy of New York's constitution from 1777. This Web site also has many other documents relating to colonial history and the founding of the United States.

QUOTE SOURCES

CHAPTER ONE

p. 15 "seeming...coming." Jameson, J. Franklin. *Narratives of New Netherland, 1609-1664*. Reprint. New York: Barnes and Noble, 1959, p. 18; "we suppose... riches." http://www.win.tue.nl/ ~engels/discovery/verrazzano.html.

CHAPTER TWO

p. 27 "kettles...small wares." Shorto, Russell. *The Island at the Center of the World*. New York: Doubleday, 2004, p. 56; "the population...children." Jameson, J. Franklin. *Narratives of New Netherland, 1609-1664*. Reprint. New York: Barnes and Noble, 1959, p. 88; "in no...with them." Jameson, p. 88; p. 28 "make... grain." Rink, Oliver A. *Holland on the Hudson: An Economic and Social History of Dutch New York*. Ithaca: Cornell University Press, 1986, p. 150; "Then New...flourish." Rink, p. 150; p. 30 "Before the...are now." Cantwell, Anne-Marie and Dianna diZerega Wall. *Unearthing Gotham: The Archaeology of New York City*. New Haven: Yale University Press, 2001, p. 143.

CHAPTER THREE

p. 36 "commanders...or not." Jameson, J. Franklin. *Narratives of New Netherland, 1609-1664*. Reprint. New York: Barnes and Noble, 1959, p. 214; p. 37 "dwellings... deserted places." Rink, Oliver A. *Holland on the Hudson: An Economic and Social History of Dutch New York*. Ithaca: Cornell University Press, 1986, p. 221; "almost all...and the like." Jameson, p. 330; p. 42 "In his...name of Manhattan." Kammen, Michael. *Colonial New York*. New York: Oxford University Press, 1975, p. 72; p. 43 "the best...in America." Shorto, Russell. *The Island at the Center of the World*. New York: Doubleday, 2004, p. 307.

CHAPTER FOUR

p. 48 "as soon as...on hand." Venema, Janny. *Beverwijck: A Dutch Village on the American Frontier, 1652-1664*. Albany: State University of New York Press, 2003, p. 294; "provide...New Netherland." Venema, p. 294; p. 51 "true...property." Shorto, Russell. *The Island at the Center of the World*. New York: Doubleday, 2004, p. 273; "such privileges...province." Shorto, p. 273.

CHAPTER FIVE

p. 57 "that the ...Royal family." http://www.newsday.com/community/guide/ lihistory/ny-history-hs320a,0,5781435.story; p. 59 "in the...disorder possible." Kammen, Michael. *Colonial New York*. New York: Oxford University Press, 1975, p. 98; p. 63 "a parcel...people." Judd, Jacob and Irwin H. Polishook, eds. *Aspects of Early New York Society and Politics*. Tarrytown: Sleepy Hollow Restorations, 1974, p. 73.

CHAPTER SIX

p. 68 "that the...account whatsoever." Richter, Daniel K. *The Ordeal of the Longhouse: The Peoples of the Iroquois League in the Era of European Civilization*. Chapel Hill: University of North Carolina Press, 1992, pp. 226-227; p. 69 "who received...to the support." Bonomi, Patricia U. *A Factious People: Politics and Society in Colonial New York*. New York: Columbia University Press, 1971, p. 86; p. 70 "SLAVERY...[placed] on." Lustig, Mary Lou. *Privilege and Prerogative: New York's Provincial Elite, 1710-1776*. Madison, New Jersey: Fairleigh Dickinson University Press, 1995, p. 47; p. 71 "It is not...the truth." http://www.law.umkc.edu/faculty/projects/ ftrials/zenger/zengeraccount.html.

CHAPTER SEVEN

p. 79 "...[the streets]...stories high." Kammen, Michael. *Colonial New York*. New York: Oxford University Press, 1975, p. 290; pp. 80-81 "Three or four...or longer." McKee, Samuel Jr. *Labor in Colonial New York, 1664-1776*. Reprint. Port Washington, New York: Ira J. Friedman, Inc., 1963, p. 28; p. 81 "We...pay...of it." Moynihan, Ruth Barnes, et al, eds. *Second to None: A Documentary History of American Women*. Vol. 1. Lincoln: University of Nebraska Press, 1993, p. 122; "some...of fire." Lustig, Mary Lou. *Privilege and Prerogative: New York's Provincial Elite, 1710-1776*. Madison, New Jersey: Fairleigh Dickinson University Press, 1995, p. 140; p. 87 "...they [the slaves]...[plan together]." Hofstadter, Richard, and Michael Wallace, eds. *American Violence: A Documentary History*. New York: Vintage Press, 2002, p. 188.

CHAPTER EIGHT

p. 90 "openly threatened...and country." Hoermann, Alfred R. *Cadwallader Colden: A Figure of the American Enlightenment*. Westport: Greenwood Press, 2002, p. 180; p. 97 "murder...of the town." Commager, Henry Steele, and Richard B. Morris, eds. *The Spirit of Seventy-Six*. New York: Harper and Row, 1967, p. 737; pp. 97-98 "Good God...day lose!" Fleming, Thomas. *Liberty!: The American Revolution*. New York: Viking, 1997, p. 189; p. 98 "leaving... flames." Commager, p. 1020; p. 101 "the prosperity...firmly united." Hamilton, Alexander, James Madison, and John Jay. *The Federalist Papers*. New York: New American Library, 1961; p. 102 "additional...property." Hamilton, Alexander, James Madison, and John Jay.

Index

ABOUT THE AUTHOR
AND CONSULTANT

MICHAEL BURGAN has been writing about colonial and Revolutionary America, immigration, religion, famous Americans, sports, and many other subjects for children and young adults for more than 10 years. His work has been published in *The New York Times*, *Sports Illustrated for Kids*, and by National Geographic. A former writer for Weekly Reader Corporation, Burgan has developed online resources and produced educational materials to be used by teachers in the classroom. He is also a playwright and currently lives in Chicago, Illinois.

TIMOTHY J. SHANNON is an Associate Professor of History at Gettysburg College in Pennsylvania. He received his Ph.D. from Northwestern University. Shannon's recent publications include books and articles on the early government of the New York colony and relations between the British and Indians in early America. His book *Indians and Colonists at the Crossroads of Empire: The Albany Congress of 1754* won a Distinguished Book Award prize in 2000. Shannon makes his home in Frederick, Maryland.

ILLUSTRATION CREDITS